STEAM MEMORIES: 1950's – 1960's

No. 10: SOUTHERN PART 1

The South Eastern & Central Division

Copyright Book Law Publications 2009

ISBN 978-1-907094-53-8

INTRODUCTION

The area under review in this album encompasses the former territory of the London, Brighton & South Coast Railway and the South Eastern & Chatham Railway which, at Grouping, became the Central and South-Eastern sections of the Southern Railway. The political boundaries are basically Kent and both halves of Sussex.

The period covered is from 1954 to 1960 and the work of two different photographers, Don Beecroft and Keith Pirt, both now having sadly passed on, have been used to present the various views.

The period chosen covers the era when British Railways was trying desperately to rebuild the business from the halcyon pre-war days whilst struggling to modernise a vast and somewhat run-down and worn-out railway system. Featured are some of the ancient locomotives and rolling stock which BR kept going whilst maintaining a creditable service in what was one of the country's busiest commuter areas. We show big and small, from the mighty Bulleid Pacifics to the tiny four and six-coupled tank engines which surprisingly outlasted many 'modern' designs.

Besides touching on the historical side of the locations, routes, trains and locomotives, we have taken a brief look at how these two Sections of the Southern worked during the transition from steam to electric main line haulage. It was, for many places, a time when services got better but for other more remote areas it was a time of loss as BR closed branch after branch and line after line.

Hopefully this album captures the essence of the period and presents some new and interesting views and facts for the reader.

(*Cover*) **See page 28.**

(*Title page*) **Maunsell L1 4-4-0 No.31787 enters West St Leonards station from the Hastings direction with a local service from Ashford to Tonbridge on Tuesday 27th July 1954. A porter drags what appears to be a heavy and awkward sack towards the area of the platform where he anticipates that the trains guards compartment will arrive. Both driver and fireman are looking out from the cab to spot any hazard whilst passengers start moving towards the platform edge and the soon to be stationary train. Off to the right of this picture, behind the station buildings, was the engine shed known as St Leonards West Marina - a name more befitting a tranquil area by the sea shore perhaps rather than a bustling engine shed. The line from Lewes and Eastbourne to Hastings runs behind the concrete buildings at the platform end and it was near to the engine shed that a station of the same name was opened by the London, Brighton & South Coast Railway in 1882. The LB&SC had in fact established a station here in 1846 but the West Marina name did not appear until 1870 when, at the same time, the SER named their station Warrior Square. This station was opened in 1887 by the South Eastern to supplement the Warrior Square establishment beyond the tunnel and offer an alternative to the general public. Both former SER stations are still open but the Brighton station was closed in July 1967. *KRP - 12H.8.1.***

Printed and bound by The Amadeus Press, Cleckheaton, West Yorkshire

First published in the United Kingdom by Book Law Publications, 382 Carlton Hill, Nottingham, NG4 1JA

VICTORIA

Looking nothing less than immaculate, 'Britannia' No.70004 WILLIAM SHAKESPEARE departs Platform 8 at Victoria station with the Down *GOLDEN ARROW* on 24th July 1954. The Pacific was a regular performer on this, the Stewarts Lane No.4 Duty, and the *NIGHT FERRY* too, along with No.70014 IRON DUKE. The locomotive names would, perhaps, not go un-noticed by foreign visitors using the service. Certainly the great British writer would be known to many if not most but the nick-name of the victor at Waterloo might not be that well known outside of these shores. Perhaps subtlety was the name of the game and the tongue-in-cheek approach, if it was ever intended that these locomotives should work these services from the outset, would not offend the majority of visitors. The arrows fitted to the smoke deflectors had been especially made for the 'Brits' because those used on the air-smooth casing of the Bullied Pacifics were too long but when the SR Pacifics began their rebuilding the small arrows came into their own again. Note that the tender is not spilling over with coal - the short working undertaken by No.70004 down to the south coast did not warrant a tenderful of fuel and there was probably enough left in the bunker for the return journey too (but see Folkestone feature). During February 1954 one of the Ashford-built main line diesel electric locomotives, 10202, took over both the *GA* and *NF* workings for a week but though completed without any real hitches, the diesels did not materialise at a future date and steam worked these important trains until electric traction took over in 1961. The last steam hauled Down and Up trains ran on 11th June 1961 and was hauled to Dover and back by rebuilt 'West Country' Pacific No.34100 APPLEDORE, turned-out, as usual, in the 73A tradition - immaculately. *KRP - 7H.8.3.*

The endless activity at a busy station like Victoria was a magnet for many enthusiasts especially those from the north of the country who were making an all-too-rapid visit to the area in the hope of bagging as many engines as possible. For those without shed permits the platform end was a must but for those with the priceless documents it was a wrench to have to leave the station when so much was happening. Here on the Eastern Section area of the terminus on 24th July 1954 we have C class 0-6-0 No.31294 performing empty carriage duties or station pilot whilst on the right 'Merchant Navy' No.35027 PORT LINE waits for departure with another boat train working. In the background is a vintage electric unit which would not have attracted too much attention from the majority in those heady days of wall-to-wall steam. Working in a station such as Victoria was a somewhat dangerous occupation for certain members of the BR work force, footplatemen and the like were constantly coupling or detaching rolling stock but because of all the conductor rails flanking virtually every track, tasks such as that required that staff have their wits about them at all times, something we take for granted even now, although locomotive hauled stock is something of a rarity on the modern railway. *KRP - 7H.8.2.*

A study of PORT LINE in its virtual as-built condition, although by now it is on its fourth livery change having been painted in lined Brunswick green during late 1953. That green was to cover the not very successful BR Standard blue which had been applied to many of the class during the three years 1949 to 1951. No.35027 was given the blue livery in April 1950, its one year old coat of malachite green disappearing for ever; when initially put into traffic, its livery was unlined malachite green on account that it was not coupled to the correct tender, however when a 6,000 gallon tender was eventually coupled in April 1949, both engine and tender got the full lining treatment too. For the first fourteen months of its life, this Pacific worked from Bournemouth shed but in March 1950 it left the *BELLE* behind and transferred to Stewarts Lane to take a hand in working the prestige trains on the Eastern Section. In July 1954 the 'MN' was due to undergo a General overhaul and that event was arranged for the end of the summer workings when its presence would not be missed too much at 73A. No.35027 moved back to the Western Section in June 1955, again to Bournemouth shed from where it worked until overtaken by events in 1966. Its six month long storage at Eastleigh, then purchase by a certain scrap metal merchant in Barry secured its future and the rest, as they say - is history. The train headed by PORT LINE is bound for Dover (Marine) and was possibly a relief working. Like much of the traffic handled by BR, including the number of boat trains to Dover and Folkestone, seasonal popularity played a major role and reliefs during the summer could be balanced against cancelled sailings and even low patronage during the winter. Of the three 'Merchant Navy' Pacifics allocated to Stewarts Lane, hindsight now shows that they were under-utilised because the amount of traffic requiring their services was not really there. Like certain trains they hauled, they were something of a luxury on the South Eastern section. In an article in the *Railway Magazine* of 1956, H.P.White reminded us that it was long ago stated that '...there were ninety ways of reaching Dover from London without reversing...' I wonder which route this train was taking? *KRP - 7H.8.1.*

Long term shed pilot P class 0-6-0T No.31557 stables for the weekend at Stewarts Lane on Saturday 24th July 1954. This diminutive tank engine was one of a pair allocated to 73A at this time, No.31555 being the other. The class first appeared in February 1909 in the shape of No.1556 (31556) which, along with our friend here, became the advance party of a class which was to eventually number just eight engines. Intended for push-pull working, the little six-coupled engines soon proved their unreliability for those duties but they found employment at Dover docks and as pilots at some of the larger engine sheds. Of the eight, which were all intact and working in 1954, three could be found at Brighton, whilst the other three resided at Dover. Miraculously, and it does not require 'A' levels in Maths to work this one out, 50% of the class were preserved - four out of the eight - something that lots of former Great Western classes can't even begin to emulate!! Alas, No.31557 did not make it into preservation, being condemned perhaps too soon in September 1957. No doubt about it, the Class P 0-6-0 tank engines had 'appeal' for some people and that phenomenon occurred early-on in the world of the preserved steam locomotives, with the last of the four being secured shortly after withdrawal in June 1961. Amazing. The British Railways WD 'Austerity' 2-8-0 class consisted 733 members. Most of those had distinguished wartime service overseas under their belts. BR enginemen thrashed and abused them but they kept going and could be relied upon to do the job, no matter what. They were cheap too (in scrap metal terms) but they had no cuddly 'appeal' like these little chaps (or were they ladies?), were nearly always dirty but they kept BR freight on the move from 1948 to 1967 (and that does not include the war years and the immediate post-war period) without any recognition whatsoever. When these little chaps were tucked-up in their home sheds, the WD 2-8-0 was busy, as usual, through the small hours hauling coal for industry and basically keeping us warm at home in the days before central heating. Anyway, the upshot is - not one of the seven hundred and thirty-three BR WD 'Austerity' 2-8-0s was chosen for preservation. A great shame indeed took place. *KRP - 8H.8.1.*

READING

At the outer north-western limit of our geographical boundary is Reading where the SE&CR established a solid base on which to funnel traffic around London in a southerly direction towards their own territory south and east of the capital. The SE&CR absorbed the Reading, Reigate & Guildford Railway in 1852, the RR&GR having got to Reading in 1849. Besides having their own passenger (Reading South) and goods station, they built an engine shed which remained independent from its larger Western Region neighbour right into British Railways days and had its own code - 70E. Known as Reading South, like the station, the shed allocation was never large in numbers but locomotives such as this D class 4-4-0, No.31075, became the 'bread and butter' of the line to Guildford and all points east. On 29th July 1954 a pair of these Wainwright veterans were still in residence - just - Ashford built No.31488 being the other, a far cry from earlier in the year when five of their number were allocated. Since then the other three had retreated to Guildford or Tonbridge. This engine too, one of the Dubs examples from 1903, was about to do that and by the end of the month would have transferred to Guildford. This left No.31488 to follow on to Guildford which it did at the end of the summer services in 1955. No.31075 is standing at the western end of the shed yard whilst the other 4-4-0 was stabled out of picture alongside the tall signal box on the left of the frame. The elevated Western Region main line overlooks the Reading SR yard. Reading (South) station closed in September 1965, its services diverted into a new bay platform at Reading (General). *KRP - 14H.8.6.*

The eastern aspect of Reading South in July 1956 with Guildford based D class No.31737 on the nearest road and with what appears to be an S15 behind. The 4-4-0 had only a couple of months operational life left before withdrawal but others would take its place for as long as the Reading shed required. Built by the South Eastern in 1875 to replace an earlier two road building, this three-road through shed was rebuilt by British Railways shortly after Nationalisation; the main part of the rebuild consisted the gables which are already fairly soot stained, and the roof cladding. The engine shed had virtually wound down to closure on 6th April 1964 but locomotives were still stabling there until September 1965. The pre-Grouping designs had long gone by then and only Type 3 diesels, with steam represented by the occasional N or U 2-6-0, would use the place. The depot became an outstation of Guildford shed long before closure and in 1960 it was shown as such, having lost its code. When the 'Schools' class lost work in the wake of the Kent Coast electrification, and the Hastings line modernisation, they found secondary employment on the Reading-Redhill services and therefore began to turn up at Reading from 1961 but their days were numbered too as withdrawals began to take a toll on the V class 4-4-0s. During the period when Reading South turntable was being repaired in April 1961, M7 class 0-4-4Ts were pressed into service on the Redhill-Reading trains from 8th April but by the 15th they had been replaced by tender engines because, apparently, they could not keep time and made a mess of the whole affair. *DHB - 7.*

GUILDFORD

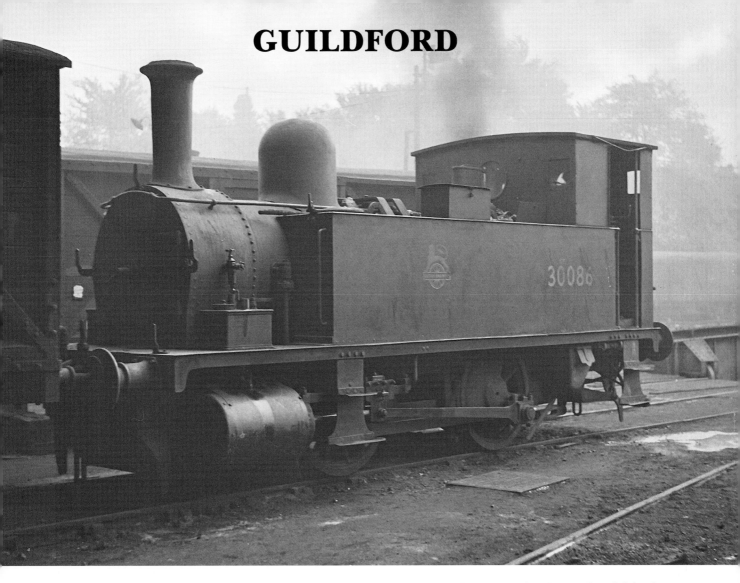

B4 class 0-4-0T No.30086 is pictured at Guildford shed in July 1954 whilst en route from Bournemouth to Dover where it joined younger brother No.30084, which had been resident at 74C and working the dock lines since its transfer from Plymouth Friary during the autumn of 1951. After a year working beneath the white cliffs No.30086 returned to Guildford and decided to stay to work the shed pilot duties which it undertook until withdrawn in February 1959. A shed pilot was very necessary at Guildford because access to the semi-roundhouse, and its seven road straight shed extension, was via the turntable. A small locomotive was ideal for the job of extricating lame or 'dead' locomotives from the depths of the shed for moving elsewhere. Before the purchase of the 'USA' tanks by the Southern Railway for working the lines within Southampton docks, this engine, along with thirteen other B4 tanks undertook that work and whilst doing so carried the name HAVRE - the others also carried names after the ports served by shipping from Southampton. However, as the 0-4-0T engines were relieved of their duties at Southampton, their names were unceremoniously removed. Miraculously only two of these little four-coupled tanks survived the British Railways scrapmen. *KRP - 13H.8.1.*

It was never the intention of this album to restrict the pre-Group locomotive classes illustrated to those which had their origins at Ashford or Brighton so in this view at Guildford in July 1954 we show former London & South Western L12 No.30434. The 4-4-0 was by now the last of its once twenty strong class and, the only one to reach fifty years of age. The L12 class was basically a larger boiler version of the perhaps more well known but nevertheless longer-lived T9 class. No.30434 was no stranger at Guildford having been allocated to the shed during the immediate post-Nationalisation period. In July 1954 it was on the books at Eastleigh but just prior to withdrawal in March 1955, it transferred to Guildford for its final few months of life. Coupled to one of the large eight-wheeled tenders when new, this engine lost it shortly after BR came into being and ended up with this lighter six-wheel type which it took to withdrawal. Eastleigh have already removed the shedplate, perhaps in anticipation of its 'official' transfer to 70C. The 4-4-0 is standing alongside the coaling stage which, due to severe site restrictions at Guildford, was sited some distance to the east of the engine shed opposite the London end of the station platforms. The stage did in fact stand on the site of the original Guildford engine shed which was replaced by the semi-roundhouse shed on the west side of Farnham road bridge in 1887. Guildford was unique on the Southern in that it was the only station where trains of the three main constituents of the Southern Railway - L&SWR, LB&SCR, SECR - regularly worked before Grouping. *KRP - 13H.8.2.*

E4 class 0-6-2T No.32468 runs onto the turntable at Horsham roundhouse in July 1954. The open roundhouse engine shed was not common in the United Kingdom by Grouping. The Midland Railway, the North Eastern , and the Great Western were all exponents of roundhouses for locomotive stabling, circular at first, and enclosed, but latterly they were square in profile, their interiors being more like cathedrals in dimension. One of the grandest open circular roundhouses was the London & South Western double turntable shed at Nine Elms but that only lasted until 1909. Circular roundhouses with open turntables were therefore rare in the 20th Century with the likes of Guildford, Inverness, Kittybrewster and St Blazey being perhaps the most famous of their ilk to survive into BR ownership, but they all had different origins. Horsham was built by the LB&SCR who erected a similar, though smaller, structure at Eastbourne. Both places were attractive and had more than a passing resemblance to the hundreds of circular roundhouses erected by the railroads of the United States. This shed was erected in 1896 and initially consisted ten stalls radiating off the turntable but just five years later a further eight stalls were added which created a building which enclosed the turntable for two-thirds of its circumference. Closed to steam in July 1959, the roundhouse remained open for other motive power until the summer of 1964 after which it was demolished. The Eastbourne shed dated from 1876 and consisted just eight radiating roads but it was replaced in 1911 by a straight shed sited some distance away. Perhaps the LB&SC brush with circular roundhouses was a short-lived affair - thirty-five years in the Eastbourne case - but they were aesthetically pleasing to look at. However, they had a 'down side' like all roundhouse sheds in that if the turntable was put out of commission, then the whole shed was out of action too. The E4 was one of nine of the class allocated to Horsham at this time. The former LB&SCR engine, along with the rest of the seventy strong class, once carried a name which in this case was MIDHURST (was this engine shedded at either of the two different sheds at that place before closure by the Southern?). Note the engine had no BR insignia on the side tank, presumably as a result that no such transfers were available during its last major overhaul and repaint. It left Horsham in early 1955 for Brighton shed and was eventually followed by the other E4s. Surviving until 1963, No.32468 was amongst the small handful which saw the class made extinct that year. *KRP - 13H.8.4.*

The outer yard at Horsham shed in late July 1954 with a couple of M7s hogging the scene. No.30038 and 30051 were part of a complement of six allocated to this depot. Their appearance bodes well for the cleaning staff who would probably double up as coal stage 'operatives' when required. The stage is typical of the period, built of lightweight materials offering minimal protection from the elements. A heavy duty curtain slung across the opening probably offered some protection during inclement weather, especially south-westerly's. Construction of the building is plain to see with the original ten-road section on the left of the picture. The brickwork and design of the extension appear to match even down to the round openings in the gables. Roof construction is simple enough and besides the central vents created by the ridge covering, there is single chimney like vent over each road approximating where the engine chimney would be positioned. From a modelling standpoint this shed could be a dream to create, certainly a long term project for the average modeller. However, some would say it would be a nightmare on account of the turntable being required for every movement in and out of the roundhouse - brilliant. The other down side is that you would have to model LBSC, SR or BR(SR) or be completely freelance. By any account it would be an attractive model and, apparently, diesels used the place for a while. *KRP - 13H.8.3.*

12

THREE BRIDGES

Another former LB&SCR engine shed in Sussex was Three Bridges Junction (BR code 75E) which by some coincidence had, during its years as a steam centre from 1848 to 1964, had three separate engine sheds. This building is the last of them and was a three-road brick structure with a proper northlight facing roof. The tracks ran through the shed to a headshunt. In late July 1954 this magnificent K class 2-6-0 was one of seven of the seventeen strong class allocated to this depot. Brighton shed had the others, except for No.32349 which was at Fratton. Intended to work the heavy goods trains on the old LB&SC, they soon proved capable of easily working passenger trains too so that over the years they have come to be regarded as mixed traffic engines. A number of BR steam locomotives classes suffered from near en bloc condemnations but none more so than these capable 2-6-0s which were withdrawn virtually en masse at the end of 1962 for no other reason as to, apparently, balance some accounting scam which had full official backing. The chances of a whole class suddenly being unserviceable at a stroke (of a pen) was something only politicians and accountants could make up but it did happen in the crazy Sixties when the rush to rid British Railways of steam was in full swing. Note the broken water column on the left - was it ever replaced? C2X 0-6-0 No.32528 was another Brighton product residing at Three Bridges, ten other C2X were allocated here in July 1954. Is that LMS 4MT No.42066 with its back to us inside the shed? or was it either of the other two 2-6-4T allocated to 75E at this time, Nos.42092 and 42093. Just before the SR batch of Fairburn tanks left the Region for good at the end of 1959, Three Bridges shed took seven of them in. *KRP - 13H.8.6.* 13

This rear aspect of Three Bridges shed shows off the elevated water tank and its associated sand house beneath, both joined to a tall chimney. As already mentioned, this was the third of the engine sheds at this junction and was opened in 1911 after a two year delay during which a temporary facility was created in the junction between the Brighton line and route to Horsham. For such a small depot (mainly in terms of allocation but also in extent), 75E was well equipped and laid out, with a coal stage and a 60ft turntable. The contents of the tender of the 0-6-0 appear to be the dreaded briquettes, which BR had to take alongside the coal ration it was allocated. This was July 1954 and the British coal industry had still not reached its extraction targets for good quality and large coal, hence the brick shaped substitute made up from slack and an unknown glue which held it all together - mechanisation at the coal face was excellent for winning the coal but at a cost in quality and size. After closure in June 1964 the Three Bridges engine shed was used to stable diesel locomotives for a number of years, then wagon repair was carried out but rationalisation eventually caught up with the facility and demolition took place. *KRP - 13H.8.7.*

BRIGHTON

The shed yard at Brighton could get quite congested at times as can be seen in the background, at the station end, but 'West Country' No.34045 OTTERY ST. MARY has plenty of room in this late afternoon view in 1955. Part of the Brighton allocation from 1951 to 1958, this Pacific looked very much the Kitmaster model. Rebuilt in 1958, its withdrawal in June 1964 saw it purchased by Woodham's at Barry but, No.34045 was one of the early arrivals at that famous yard and was cut up in May 1965 before all the fuss began. *KRP - 115F. 7.*

One of the gems found at Brighton in 1954 was Stroudley A1X 'Terrier' No.377S turned out in original LB&SCR livery as the **BRIGHTON WORKS** shunter. Here on 28th July 1954 the little 0-6-0T is doing a spot of shunting and earning its keep in semi-retirement as a Departmental locomotive. The engine was treated to this Stroudley yellow repaint in 1947 at, appropriately, Brighton shops, on its transfer from the Hayling Island branch (Fratton shed) as SR No.2635. Much of its work at Brighton now consisted back and forth trips between the goods yard and the locomotive works with vans full of stores - its daily mileage rarely getting into double figures. This was a far-cry from pre-Grouping days when, on some Brighton push and pull jobs, the little 0-6-0 tanks could run up to 180 miles daily from leaving shed shortly before 6.00 a.m. and returning home just before 9.00 p.m.. Other jobs could see as many as 195 miles being clocked up by the A1X involved, although not all of those miles were revenue earning. Brighton works was fairly busy at this time and although the construction of the BR Standard Cl.4 tanks had been completed and locomotive building was finished, intermediate overhauls of anything from Bullied Pacifics to O2 tank engines was being performed alongside the inevitable scrapping of condemned engines. *KRP - 14H.8.5.*

The impressively large, though grotty-looking water softening plant, with the huge water tower alongside, dwarf the already diminutive A1X No.32662 as it stands next to the wheel hoist at Brighton engine shed in September 1960. The wheel drop is sited beneath the timber clad 'shed' in the left background. By now Brighton engine shed was slowly running down as new diesel units started to appear from all sides taking over the numerous passenger and goods services run by the steam motive power supplied by 75A. The nearby locomotive works was running down even faster with locomotive building having ceased in March 1957 and locomotive overhauls in 1958. Whatever work was carried on after that time was finished in 1964 when the works closed ending 124 years of railway history. The works at Brighton was famous for a number of locomotive designs including the Atlantics, Bulleid Pacifics, the last tank locomotive built for BR - No.80154, the first main-line diesel locomotives for BR and of course these little chaps - the 0-6-0 A1X tank engine which, in preservation have outlived the establishment responsible for their design and construction. One other 'famous' class not yet mentioned was the ill-starred 'Leader' of which the less said the better, perhaps. *DHB - 4684.*

Taking the coast line as far as Shoreham-by-Sea, then afterwards swinging on to the Steyning line, H class No.31308 passes the engine shed 18 **at Brighton as it departs from the terminus with a push-pull service to Horsham in September 1960.** *DHB - 4682.*

Another famous Brighton product was the Marsh Atlantic No.32424 BEACHY HEAD - the last Atlantic to work in Britain. The date is 28th July 1954, a time when four other members of the original six H2 class were also still active. The 4-4-2, standing on Brighton shed yard, does not appear to be particularly looked after just now but things would get better for the engine before its demise. The main duties of the class during BR days was to work the Brighton-Bournemouth passenger trains and the Newhaven boat trains. All five were shedded at Brighton but at least one and sometimes three were sub-shedded at Newhaven for the latter job. All except this engine had been condemned by October 1956 so No.32424 became something of a celebrity amongst enthusiasts and was being called upon to perform on specials, besides doing its normal work on the Bournemouth trains, until it too was condemned on the evening of Sunday 13th April 1958. Earlier that day it had hauled an RCTS special from Victoria to Newhaven. The similarity between the LB&SCR H2 and the Great Northern C1 was not surprising really as Marsh, before taking charge at Brighton, had been Chief Assistant Mechanical Engineer at Doncaster under Ivatt. It is, perhaps, the reason why this engine was not preserved in the National Collection. *KRP - 14H.8.4.*

SHOREHAM

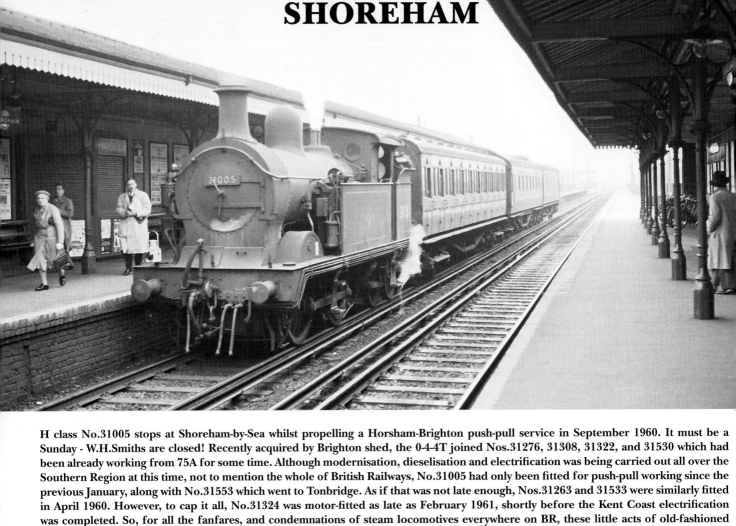

H class No.31005 stops at Shoreham-by-Sea whilst propelling a Horsham-Brighton push-pull service in September 1960. It must be a Sunday - W.H.Smiths are closed! Recently acquired by Brighton shed, the 0-4-4T joined Nos.31276, 31308, 31322, and 31530 which had been already working from 75A for some time. Although modernisation, dieselisation and electrification was being carried out all over the Southern Region at this time, not to mention the whole of British Railways, No.31005 had only been fitted for push-pull working since the previous January, along with No.31553 which went to Tonbridge. As if that was not late enough, Nos.31263 and 31533 were similarly fitted in April 1960. However, to cap it all, No.31324 was motor-fitted as late as February 1961, shortly before the Kent Coast electrification was completed. So, for all the fanfares, and condemnations of steam locomotives everywhere on BR, these little acts of old-fashioned railway working were still being created. No.31005 carried on in that role until September 1963 when the inevitable took place. It ended up in a private scrapyard at Queenborough, Kent. A couple of M7s were tried on these services in 1960 but with such disastrous results that they were taken off the work, probably the reason why the H class engines were motor fitted so late on. In March 1961 Ivatt Cl.2MT 2-6-2Ts, allocated to Brighton shed, were introduced to the Steyning line services. When the Brighton-Horsham p&p ended in early 1964, three-car diesel units ran the service completely from 4th May, apparently to p&p timings until the summer timetable was introduced. But the Steyning line was closed to passenger services just a few years later in March 1966. The last push-pull service on the SR were hauled/propelled by Bournemouth based M7 class 0-4-4Ts on the Swanage and Lymington branches in May 1964. The LB&SCR station (London & Brighton Railway at the time of opening) opened here at 3.00 p.m. on Monday 11th May 1840. Built by the London & Brighton Railway, the station and its six mile branch from the Brighton terminus was the first part of the railway to be opened for traffic. Until 1845 Shoreham was the western limit of the coast railway but during that year contractors continued building westward and the line reached Portsmouth in June 1847. The station is still in business having seen goodness knows how many classes and types of steam locomotive, with both diesel and electric traction to boot latterly. *DHB - 4679.*

LEWES

Its raining again. Well it is still British Summer Time! BR Standard Cl.4 No.80154 runs into Platform 7 at Lewes with a Tunbridge Wells (Central)-Brighton train in early September 1960. The 2-6-4T was one of eighteen allocated to Brighton shed at this time but this engine was not just another BR Standard tank. It was to prove to be the last of its type but it nearly did not get built at all. When, in May 1956, the completion of the Class 4 tanks was in sight, it was decided that the last five, Nos.80150 to 80154, would be cancelled (a further fifteen Nos.80155 to 80169 had already been cancelled). But, most of the materials and parts required for their completion was already made or to hand so, after a period of delay, it was then decided to go ahead and build the last five rather than 'waste' the various parts and keep them as spares which would probably never be used anyway. So, the last five came out of Brighton shops three months behind their scheduled completion date. No.80154 was thus released to traffic as the last British Railways 2-6-4T on Tuesday 26th March 1957. Not only that distinction occurred but its departure from the works at Brighton marked the end of locomotive construction there so it was appropriate to allocate the engine to 75A along with Nos.80145 to 80153. In June 1963, with diesels and electrics rapidly taking over the work, No.80154 was transferred to Feltham, then in November 1964 it moved to Nine Elms. Withdrawn on Sunday 2nd April 1967, the Class 4 went for scrap to a yard in Newport, South Wales a few months later, largely forgotten for the two significant milestones it's building had created. *DHB - 4690.*

'Battle of Britain' No.34055 FIGHTER PILOT gets away from Lewes with a Brighton to London (Victoria) working in September 1960. The train is signalled for Eridge, Oxted and Purley before it peels off into the maze of lines around south London. Acquired by Brighton shed from Salisbury depot in March 1960, the 'BB' was effectively on its last posting and would continue to work from Brighton until withdrawn on 22nd June 1963. It was never rebuilt and had the distinction of being not only the first unrebuilt SR Pacific to be withdrawn but also the first to be condemned. It was also one of the few to be cut up at Eastleigh. When it went into traffic in February 1947, as 21C155, it did not carry a name - the Southern Railway was still picking and choosing those. However, on Friday 19th September 1947, at Brighton station, in the company of Nos.21C153 and 21C167, it was named by none other than Group Captain Bader. No.21C153 was named SIR KEITH PARK by the Knight himself, and 21C167 was named TANGMERE by a Wing Commander Clouston. Note the lone flower tub decorating the rain soaked platform - at least pride in one's station was encouraged in 1960. *DHB - 4688.*

TONBRIDGE

In April 956, two former LB&SCR E3 0-6-2Ts, Nos.32456 and 32454, are captured when stored 'out the back' of Tonbridge engine shed whilst the Q1 alongside receives attention. Although the Q1 was usefully left bereft of running plates and splashers, which might ordinarily have got in the way for oiling purposes, the lack of said running plate created problems for fitters and it was necessary to have sets of ladders at SR depots for the purpose of attending to anything above frame level. The same can be said of the Bullied Pacifics in their original 'spam can' form but many of the depots which had those engines allocated had mobile platforms where both fitters and cleaners could work in relative safety and with some room to manoeuvre. Both tank engines were products of Brighton and came into traffic in May 1895. By now you would imagine that they were living on borrowed time but that was not the case because BR got two more years work out of these two. Designed initially for goods haulage, these engines carried names in the Brighton tradition before Grouping; No.32454 being STORRINGTON whilst 32456 was ALDINGBOURNE. No.32456 was a long time resident of Tonbridge and was withdrawn there in August 1959. No.32454 had transferred to 74D from Bricklayers Arms in January 1950 and returned there in March 1957 to work out its final year at the London depot. *KRP - 118F.7.* 23

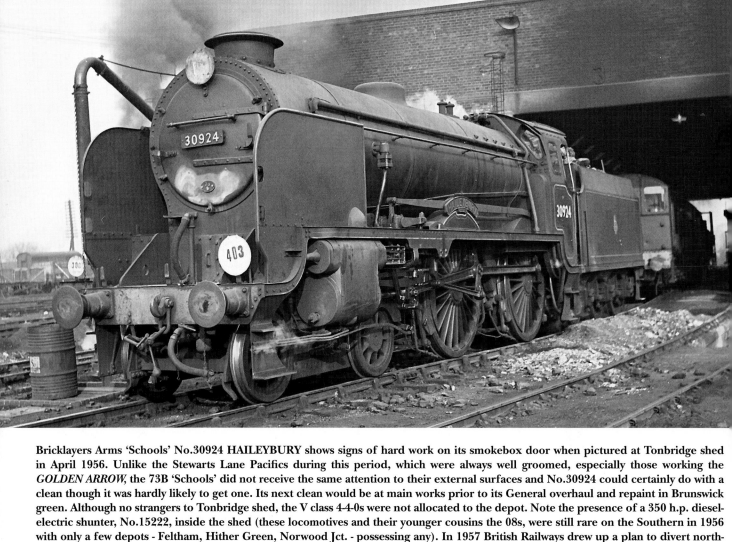

Bricklayers Arms 'Schools' No.30924 HAILEYBURY shows signs of hard work on its smokebox door when pictured at Tonbridge shed in April 1956. Unlike the Stewarts Lane Pacifics during this period, which were always well groomed, especially those working the *GOLDEN ARROW*, the 73B 'Schools' did not receive the same attention to their external surfaces and No.30924 could certainly do with a clean though it was hardly likely to get one. Its next clean would be at main works prior to its General overhaul and repaint in Brunswick green. Although no strangers to Tonbridge shed, the V class 4-4-0s were not allocated to the depot. Note the presence of a 350 h.p. diesel-electric shunter, No.15222, inside the shed (these locomotives and their younger cousins the 08s, were still rare on the Southern in 1956 with only a few depots - Feltham, Hither Green, Norwood Jct. - possessing any). In 1957 British Railways drew up a plan to divert north-south goods traffic around London to cut down line occupation on the already congested routes within the capital. The scheme envisaged bringing trains from Cambridge across to Bletchley and then to Oxford. from there the route would take them through Didcot to Reading where the former SER line to Guildford would be used to funnel trains onto the Redhill line and on to Tonbridge where a new yard was to be created. The project envisaged improved signalling and permanent way, flyovers and chord lines at important junctions, widenings and new yards. In 1958, part of the plan began to take shape with, for instance, the flyover at Bletchley but the grand plan was never finished and except for the Bletchley work and improved signalling along part of the route, it hardly go stared. Financial constraints, for the railways, along with a fall in goods revenue because of the loss of traffic to road transport meant that the plan was shelved and finally scrapped. Fifty years on, and with the benefit of hindsight, we can see that the scheme would have worked, assuming the goods traffic had been won back. Road congestion would be less and perhaps the Chunnel route might have been different. Tonbridge never did get its modern yard and to this day the route carries virtually nothing but passenger traffic. *KRP - 118F.3.*

Having set off from Tonbridge station with a stopping train to Brighton, L1 No.31785 takes the Hastings route towards Tunbridge Wells on Tuesday 17th July 1956. On the right is the Tonbridge engine shed coal stage with Ashford-built 0-6-0 diesel No.15222 now out in the shed yard and apparently doing some work. The 4-4-0 had a rather circuitous journey to the south coast, taking in both Tunbridge Wells stations, Central and West. Next would be Groombridge before turning south onto the Eastbourne line as far as where the line diverges at Eridge. Taking the route to Uckfield in a south-westerly direction along the so-called Lavender Line to Lewes where a couple of tunnels are negotiated (the part of the route just traversed was closed long ago by BR but some sections have been re-opened by enthusiasts and developed into presevered railways). From Lewes a more westerly route through Falser and Moulsecoomb would take the train through London Road and then, passing the Brighton Locomotive works and engine shed, into the terminus at the seaside - sixteen stations in all, assuming that each had been served. *DHB - 48.*

When 0-4-4T No.31661 was condemned in September 1955, No.31666 became the last R class in existence, but only for three more months before it too got the call for scrapping. Here at Tonbridge shed on 27th July 1954 the motor-fitted veteran is looking its age but is still in employment and before its eventual retirement it would venture further afield from Tonbridge and take up work on the Brighton-Horsham services, besides those from the latter place to Guildford. Ex works, alongside the four-coupled tank, is Brighton-built K class 2-6-0 No.32352, one of the 1921-built batch which though intended for goods services turned out to be a very good mixed traffic type. The K class was the first LB&SCR design to carry the Belpaire firebox and BR classified the 2-6-0s as 4MT at first but in 1953 they were reclassified 4P5F. The cab side sheet usually carried the designation but Ashford appears to have left it off the right side of the cab but it was definately on the left side sheet. The Three Bridges based 2-6-0 had completed a month long General overhaul at Ashford on 8th July but a defect found during its running-in regime saw it return to the works from 14th to 17th. Ten days later it is back in normal traffic and is turned ready to work home via Tunbridge Wells and East Grinstead. The K class remained faithful to their Brighton roots and throughout the BR era and up to their sudden demise at the end of 1962, they worked from just three depots, Brighton, Fratton and Three Bridges with little or no swapping between sheds. The two shed buildings here date from different periods, the first shed being opened in May 1842, the other being erected in the 1860s. Both building were rebuilt by BR in the period style of 1952 with brick screen gable ends. The depot closed to steam on 17th June 1962. *KRP - 12H.8.8.*

Anyone viewing H class No.31263 standing on Tonbridge engine shed yard in early 1956, would have no idea that the 0-4-4T would be fitted out for push-pull working four years hence. Likewise they would probably have ridiculed the idea that the tank engine would survive for another eight years in BR employment. But, both of those facts did become reality. *KRP - 118F.4.*

PADDOCK WOOD

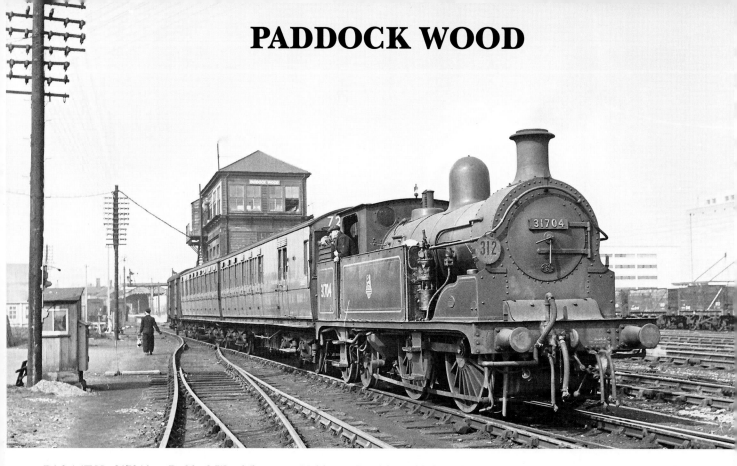

R1 0-4-4T No.31704 is at Paddock Wood (known as Maidstone Road from 1842 to 1844) on Tonbridge depot Duty No.312, which took the engine onto the Hawkhurst branch, besides trips in the opposite direction to Sevenoaks. It is autumn 1955 and this 0-4-4 motor-fitted tank has only the winter timetable to look forward to before it is consigned for scrap, however, on Easter Monday 1956, suitably cleaned and with coupling rods and buffer shanks painted white, it carried out its final duties - motor-train workings from Tonbridge as usual - before withdrawal. It was the last London, Chatham & Dover Railway design on British Railways although built some time after that railway had ceased to exist as a separate company. This view shows the engines backing into the bay at Paddock Wood to drop off the van and coach set No.723 (the first passenger vehicle is S3853S, a Brake Third in the SR scheme). Afterwards it would work onto the Hawkhurst branch with a different set of coaches. Freight traffic on the Hawkhurst branch was normally in the hands of an E4 with the R1 taking care of the passenger working, and any shunting, during the afternoon. E4 class No.32580 was temporarily allocated to the closed Hawkhurst engine shed towards the end of January 1955 when a landslide between Horsmonden and Goudhurst trapped the engine at the terminal end of the branch for three days whilst the subsidence was made good. The tank engine continued working the accessible section of the branch with road transport taking care of the 'gap'. Whilst the crews for the 'stranded' engine were taken from Tonbridge by road to Hawkhurst, coal for the engine was apparently purchased from a local merchant at the terminus goods yard. Another 'special event' in 1955 saw an RCTS rail tour *THE WEALDEN LIMITED* 'doing' the branch on 14th August as part of an extensive tour of the lines in both Kent and East Sussex. Motive power for the branch section of the tour was provided by O1 class 0-6-0 No.31048 and H class 0-4-4T No.31177, hauling eight varied coaches, including a Pullman buffet car. The gross weight of the train was 275 tons and the number of 'passengers' amounted to 275 persons. The Hawkhurst branch was described by many as a 'mountainous railway' which was something of an overstatement perhaps but by any means it was not an easy branch to work with its steep and numerous gradients. *KRP - 118F.10.*

Maunsell 'Arthur' No.30804 SIR CADOR OF CORNWALL pulls onto the Down main after a station stop at Paddock Wood in October 1955 with a stopping train for Canterbury and Ramsgate. For nearly twenty years the Southern relied on these very able 4-6-0s to work their principal passenger services and they could be found all over the railway from Devon to Kent. Introduced by the L&SWR in 1918 with Urie at the helm, the design was taken on by the Southern but the earlier engines (30736 to 30755) required some tinkering by Maunsell to make them as good as his own later 'King Arthur' design. Whilst Eastleigh was busy producing the first of Maunsell's 'King Arthur' class 4-6-0s in 1925, Nos.30453 to 30457 and 30448 to 30452, the North British Locomotive Co. were building Nos.30763 to 30792 in Glasgow at the same time. This particular batch became popularly known as the 'Scotch Arthurs'. Until 1952 the class remained intact with seventy-four engines but then withdrawals started, slowly at first but gathering momentum with each passing year and by the end of 1962 they were all gone. As mentioned earlier, No.30804 was one of the 1926 Eastleigh built batch evicted from the Central Section when the 'Brighton' was electrified in the mid-thirties'. Moving to the Western Section during the summer of 1959, the 4-6-0 was amongst the final twelve still operational at the end of 1961 but it was condemned in February 1962 and ended up in the scrap line at Ashford, one of only two N15s cut up there. Now then, how about that for a signal box! The elevated timber structure straddled the single line to the Hawkhurst branch and controlled al the movements here. Five miles to the east of Tonbridge, Paddock Wood also had a line to Maidstone branching off at the eastern end of the station. *KRP - 118F.14.*

No.31704 works the Hawkhurst branch passenger service in 1955. Note the tidy nature of the track formation at this point. The branch was opened fully to the Hawkhurst terminus on Monday 4th September 1893 by the Cranbrook & Paddock Wood Railway. Three intermediate stations were served along its length, the first, from the junction, being Horsmonden which opened nearly a year earlier on Saturday 1st October 1892; then came Hope Mill which opened on the same day and was renamed Goudhurst shortly afterwards. Goudhurst served as the terminus during the period when the contractor was pushing the line southwards and two platforms were provided. The last intermediate station was Cranbrook, which opened on the same day as the terminus. Facilities at Hawkhurst were quite lavish and besides the terminal station, a two-road engine shed was erected and sited just by the station throat. A goods shed with adjoining yard, storage sidings, four-ton capacity crane and livestock pens completed the facility. Taken over by the South Eastern in 1900, the branch thrived for many years but the trade depression between the wars saw the Southern Railway close the engine shed in 1931. At this time the population of Hawkhurst stood at 3,100 souls with as many again living within a few miles of the place. Thirty years later, on 12th June 1961, the branch, its terminus and intermediate stations all followed the fate of the engine shed and closed. Yet another section of Britain's railway system ceased to exist although some of the terminal buildings, the old engine shed in particular, were in 'other use' as late as 1995. The branch was not any easy one to work, its route through the Wealden hills ensured gradients of varying severity with 1 in 40 not being uncommon. Because of the hilly nature of the district, two of the stations, Cranbrook and Hawkhurst were situated some distance from the towns they served, the former by just under two miles and the latter by just over a mile, simply because they could not be sited any nearer. It was the original intention to build a short branch through Hartley, near Cranbrook station, to Cranbrook town (population 3,829 in 1931) but this did not materialise. Hawkhurst was a favourite destination for weekend ramblers, arriving on special excursion trains, before the outbreak of hostilities in 1939 but it was not until June 1956 that BR ran such a service again. However, even after a seventeen year gap, the train laid-on for Sunday 24th June from London (Victoria) was well patronised with eleven well-filled coaches. From London to Paddock Wood the excursion was hauled by N class No.31811 via Redhill. Two C class 0-6-0s Nos.31583 and 31590 took the train onto the branch at Paddock Wood but then had to divide it at Hawkhurst, with much delay, to get all the vehicles into the platform - the price of success! The services using the branch on 2nd May 1961 consisted H class No.31500 on the Paddock Wood passenger turns, C class No.31592 on the branch freight and what was to be the last Charing Cross-Cranbrook school special which worked onto the branch with D1 No.31749 in charge of six coaches and a van. Just before closure another ramblers' excursion consisting nine coaches and laid on from London on 28th May 1961, was worked throughout from Victoria to Hawkhurst by D1 No.31739 and E1 No.31067. However the LCGB nine-coach special of the 11th June was the very last passenger train to use the branch. Normal service trains had run the day before, beefed-up to five coaches with C class No.31588 in place of the H class tank. *KRP - 119F.4.*

ST LEONARDS

St Leonards engine shed had a reasonable stud of the 'Schools' and No.30905 TONBRIDGE stands at the south end of the shed on 27th July 1954 whilst receiving attention from an unseen fitter. The roof of the four road engine shed was rebuilt in 1948/49, the original roof dated from 1898 and years of constant use, storm, decay and apparently enemy action had taken its toll on the structure. The LB&SCR had first established locomotive facilities here about 1846 but the first shed, a two-road affair, was not provided until 1870. That building lasted until the 1890s when further accommodation was urgently required for the growing locomotive allocation at St Leonards. This four road shed, with three roads running through the eastern end, sufficed until closure although on some summer weekends the yard became extremely busy with visiting engines. Besides the eleven Class V 'Schools' allocated to this place in summer 1954 - Nos.30900 to 30910 - two more joined the complement in 1955. In November 1956 another 'V' arrived in the shape of No.30923 which effectively gave the depot (code 74E) its highest ever allocation of the popular 4-4-0 'namers' since the fourteen which resided there in November 1950. Note the Q1 tender peeping out of the shed. The Southern built 0-6-0s were never allocated to St Leonards but the Tonbridge based members of the class were regular visitors to West Marina. *KRP - 11H.8.7.*

31

'As ugly as they were powerful' was one down-to-earth description used for the Bulleid Q1 class of engine and perhaps that was correct but they certainly had something about them, just like the WD Austerity 2-8-0, which required a second look. This is No.33028 outside St Leonards shed on a sunny day in 1956 with one of the resident 'Schools' keeping it company. *KRP - 117F.13.*

As late as 27th July 1954 E class 4-4-0 No.31166 was still carrying the full word version of its current owner's title along with a front buffer beam number and shaded transfer figures to boot. This picture taken at the east end of the St Leonards shed yard reveals the engine in all its post Nationalisation glory nearly seven years after the event. It was withdrawn about ten months after this picture was captured on film so the chances are that it never did get the BR emblem on the tender nor a cast number plate on the smokebox door. However, the locomotives still looks active with a well loaded tender (and some choice coal). The Tonbridge based 4-4-0 was by now the last of its class, the penultimate member, Redhill's No.31315 being condemned earlier in the year. *KRP - 11H.8.8.*

33

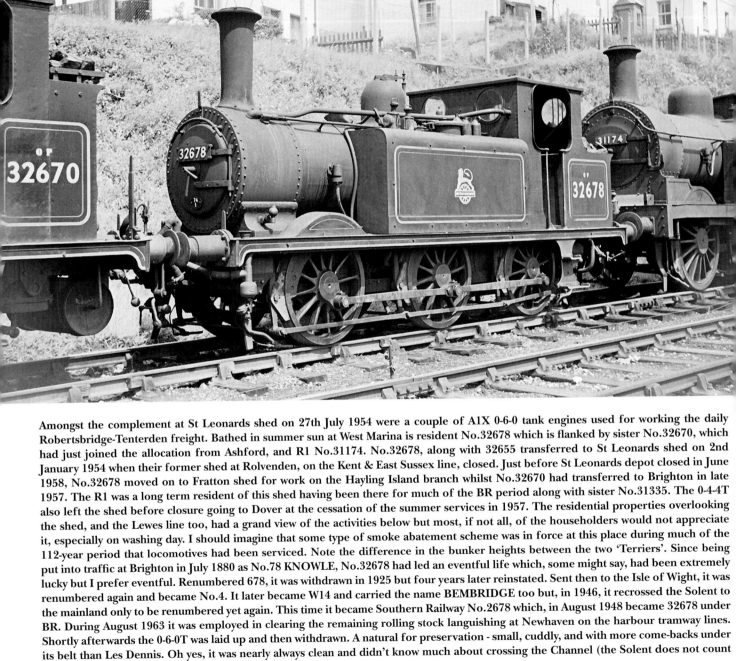

Amongst the complement at St Leonards shed on 27th July 1954 were a couple of A1X 0-6-0 tank engines used for working the daily Robertsbridge-Tenterden freight. Bathed in summer sun at West Marina is resident No.32678 which is flanked by sister No.32670, which had just joined the allocation from Ashford, and R1 No.31174. No.32678, along with 32655 transferred to St Leonards shed on 2nd January 1954 when their former shed at Rolvenden, on the Kent & East Sussex line, closed. Just before St Leonards depot closed in June 1958, No.32678 moved on to Fratton shed for work on the Hayling Island branch whilst No.32670 had transferred to Brighton in late 1957. The R1 was a long term resident of this shed having been there for much of the BR period along with sister No.31335. The 0-4-4T also left the shed before closure going to Dover at the cessation of the summer services in 1957. The residential properties overlooking the shed, and the Lewes line too, had a grand view of the activities below but most, if not all, of the householders would not appreciate it, especially on washing day. I should imagine that some type of smoke abatement scheme was in force at this place during much of the 112-year period that locomotives had been serviced. Note the difference in the bunker heights between the two 'Terriers'. Since being put into traffic at Brighton in July 1880 as No.78 KNOWLE, No.32678 had led an eventful life which, some might say, had been extremely lucky but I prefer eventful. Renumbered 678, it was withdrawn in 1925 but four years later reinstated. Sent then to the Isle of Wight, it was renumbered again and became No.4. It later became W14 and carried the name BEMBRIDGE too but, in 1946, it recrossed the Solent to the mainland only to be renumbered yet again. This time it became Southern Railway No.2678 which, in August 1948 became 32678 under BR. During August 1963 it was employed in clearing the remaining rolling stock languishing at Newhaven on the harbour tramway lines. Shortly afterwards the 0-6-0T was laid up and then withdrawn. A natural for preservation - small, cuddly, and with more come-backs under its belt than Les Dennis. Oh yes, it was nearly always clean and didn't know much about crossing the Channel (the Solent does not count in my book). No.32670 was also preserved. *KRP - 11H.8.5.*

Pioneer 'Schools' No.30900 ETON passing two other members of the class as it makes its way off shed at St Leonards in July 1956. By the start of the following summer, St Leonards had lost eleven of its 'Schools' which had transferred to Nine Elms (5), Stewarts Lane (2), Bricklayers Arms (2), and two to Ramsgate to join the other eight already in residence at that place. The transfers were simply a prelude to the closure of St Leonards and the three remaining 'Vs' had gone before the start of the 1958 summer timetable. The depot closed in June 1958 but the facilities remained in situ for visiting steam locomotives to be serviced. So ended more than one hundred and ten years of engine shed history at this place. However, it was still too early to hang out the washing in confidence. *KRP - 117F.14.*

An unidentified 'Schools' rounds the curve into West St Leonards station after exiting Bopeep tunnel with a train from Hasting to Charing Cross circa December 1955. It is just possible to see the lines of the Lewes and Eastbourne route, going off to the right, between the train and the Bopeep Junction signal box. On Saturday 7th June 1958 the last steam hauled London-Hasting express, 1.2 p.m. ex Cannon Street, was hauled by 'Schools' No.30901 WINCHESTER. The next day, after three weeks or so of gradual introduction, the specially built and narrow bodied diesel-electric multiple units took over the London-Hastings service completely and the remaining St Leonards 'Schools' moved away for good, their job done. *KRP - 118F.1.*

Amongst the last work the six-coupled goods carried out at its former home, C class No.31498 performed special duties at St Leonards engine shed on one day in April 1958 - clearing empty wagons from the coal stage now that the shed was, for all intents and purposes, closed. Official closure came in mid-June but by then the allocation had dispersed and this 0-6-0 moved on also, to Hither Green. The diesel units which took on the London services had their own shed built just west of the Marina site and long may it last. *DHB - 3433.*

ASHFORD

On arrival at Ashford station in the fifties' the first thing you would note is the Up and Down fast tracks sitting in the middle of the wide gulf between the platforms. Also of note would have been the dead straight alignment of the main line which is demonstrated for us in July 1956 by 'West Country' No.34017 ILFRACOMBE heading an Up Dover (Maritime) - London (Victoria) boat train. Although the train would be rather heavy, the gradient through Ashford, and indeed for most of the route through Kent, is fairly easy for the most part and at this particular point the Stewarts Lane based Pacific would be doing about sixty-odd miles an hour and looking to do more. This aspect of the south-east end of Ashford station reveals that two-way working was in operation on this the Up platform, the route to Hastings diverging off to the right opposition the third vehicle of the boat train. In the distance, also on this side of the main line can be seen part of the locomotive works which, in 1956, was still busy with steam locomotive repairs. On the left, Down side, of the line is a group of sidings which hide the junction to Canterbury beyond which stood the engine shed. 'WC' No.34017 was one of the elder members of its class and already it has clocked nearly eleven years service with another to notch up before heading off to Eastleigh for rebuilding in October 1957. It has always amused this writer that the names carried by the WC/BB engines meant nothing to the BR authorities once the class was complete in 1951. Much has been written about the names themselves, how they were chosen and designated. The Southern authorities thought it preferable that locomotives carrying a West Country name be allocated to what became the Western Section of BR whilst those wearing a Battle of Britain related name be allocated to the Eastern or Central sections. That indeed was the wisdom and theory behind the naming but in practice, during BR days especially, it appeared to be more of a matter of ignorance, devil-may-care or sheer mischief for the most part. ILFRACOMBE being a typical example; it was, for its first eight years working from Exmouth Junction shed serving the lines of the West Country. However, in early 1954 it was reallocated to Stewarts Lane to work over the Eastern Section as here. It remained 'on the wrong side' until January 1961 when it returned to the Western Section at Nine Elms but only because of electrification. That is one example. Another concerns 'Battle of Britain' No.34056 CROYDON which transferred to Nine Elms in June 1949 from Stewarts Lane and stayed on the Western Section until withdrawn in May 1967. There were more, dozens of them. *DHB - 47.*

Another view of the south-east end at Ashford in July 1956 with 'King Arthur' No.30804 SIR CADOR OF CORNWALL heading north on the Up fast. This nearer view of the junction affords a better aspect of the trackwork and the signals in the distance, with those for the Canterbury line and engine shed fixed to the gantry behind the parachute water tank. Note that the extra tall signal, allowing the road for the 4-6-0, is still pegged, due no doubt to the fact that the engine has only just cleared the multiple junctions. This N15 was one of the fourteen built by the Southern in 1926 for the Central Section, before the latter's electrification. All of them were coupled to six-wheel tenders and kept them throughout. When the Brighton line was electrified the 1926-built 'Arthurs' were sent to other areas of the Southern, No.30804 to the Eastern Section ending up at Ashford along with 30801, 30802, 30803 and 30805. All five were resident at 74A during most of the BR period but No.30804 moved to Dover in 1957 then over to the Western Section at Eastleigh. *DHB - 106.*

With little in the way of identification other than a fading painted number on the front bufferbeam, this is very forlorn D class 4-4-0 No.S1493 awaiting its fate in the works sidings alongside the main line on Tuesday 27th July 1954. Condemned in February, it was cut up during the week ending 25th December, and was one of four D class scrapped at Ashford during the year. For the record the others were Nos.31750 (May), 31729 (August), and 31746 also w/e 25th December. *KRP - 11H.8.3.*

A little further down the scrap line at Ashford on this last weekend of July 1954, was E class No.31315 which had been condemned during the previous March. Looking little better than S1493, it had at least managed to acquire a British Railways number on the cab side and, by the looks of the holes in the smokebox door it also carried a cast plate at some time prior to its arrival at Ashford. Both engines had been built at this works, No.31315 in April 1909 whilst S1493 was a bit longer in the tooth by six years and one month. For some reason the scrapping of locomotives at Ashford was on the slow side in 1954 with just twelve engines dealt with. No.31315 had to wait until 1955 before it was dismantled. *KRP - 11H.8.2.*

Ex works on the previous Saturday, former South Eastern R1 class No.31704 makes a pleasing sight on the shed yard at Ashford on Tuesday 27th July. Based at Tonbridge, the push-pull fitted 0-4-4T has just completed a General overhaul which took place from 8th to 24th July, including the repaint. According to works records, it had covered 109,270 since its last 'General' and because of its configuration its duties would basically make sure it did half of that mileage going forwards and the other half running backwards. However, No.31704 had only been push-pull fitted for two years up to this time so perhaps 55,000 miles per annum is expecting too much for the work it performed. This July 1954 major repair was to prove to be its last, the Kirtley designed and Ashford built veteran, albeit rebuilt by Wainwright, was withdrawn in April 1956, the last of its once fifteen strong class - age fifty-six years. In the meantime the 0-4-4T will do a couple of days running-in prior to heading home to take up its various duties which saw it working from Tonbridge to Sevenoaks, besides the Hawkhurst branch services. *KRP - 10H.8.3.*

42

Weighing in a couple of tons heavier than the R1, Wainwright's own H class 0-4-4T looked somewhat different than the R1. No.31327, photographed at Ashford shed 27th July 1954, has the distinctive 'pagoda' cab roof which endeared the class to all who came across them. The by now Ashford based engine had only been 'fitted' for push-pull working since the previous August during its short lived residence at Faversham. The main works can be seen in the background still wearing some of the camouflage applied to the structure during WW2. *KRP - 10H.8.2.*

Ashford shed coaling stage in July 1956 with St Leonards push and pull fitted H class 0-4-4T No.31519 having its small bunker filled with some rather large lumps of coal. The coaling stage was built when the engine shed was erected on this new site in 1931. Consisting of ten roads, the engine shed was constructed in concrete, the Southern's favourite building material during that period (and probably throughout its existence). Concrete was also used for the base and coaling floor of the stage but corrugated materials, supported on a lightweight frame, made up the rest of the structure. Similar structures were erected at Norwood Junction engine shed, although stout girders were used for the base and coaling floor support, Hither Green too used large girders in place of concrete but both of the latter places came a couple of years after the completion of the Ashford scheme. *DHB - 40.*

Maunsell L1 3P 4-4-0 No.31753 fills the frame of this picture taken at Ashford shed in November 1955. Of the fifteen engines in the class, five were allocated to Dover, No.31753 amongst them, five to Ashford, three to Gillingham and two were at Bricklayers Arms. All had been supplied by the North British Locomotive Co., Glasgow during March and April 1926. The L1 class was the Southern version of the South Eastern L class of which there was twenty-two in the class and dated from 1914. Those engines worked similar duties to the L1 in the same geographical area and at the end of 195 were allocated to Tonbridge (9), Ashford (6), Ramsgate (4), St Leonards (2), and one at Bricklayers Arms. Ten of the L class were made in Germany but erected at Ashford works in 1914, the others came from Beyer, Peacock later the same year. *KRP - 119F.9.*

There always seemed to be something missing when you saw a Z class 0-8-0 side-on. Nevertheless the eight members of the class looked impressive enough, especially when banking trains up the incline between St Davids and Central stations in Exeter. This is No.30952 looking for work at Ashford in November 1955. At that time 74A had another of the class allocated, No.30955 but by the end of the year Nos.30950 and 30951 had joined them from Tonbridge and Three Bridges (stored) respectively. In April 1956 No.30950 transferred to Exmouth Junction but the other three hung on at Ashford until 1959 when they too followed so that by the summer of 1959 all but one, No.30957 at Salisbury, were concentrated at Exeter. Whilst on the Ashford strength these engines worked the hump sidings (Duty 385) amongst other jobs but the coming of diesel shunters in July 1955 (13044, 13045 and 13046) saw 30952 and 30955 laid up and put into store. Later that year both engines were put through works. Three other members of the class, Nos.30950, 30951 and 30956 spent the period from mid-August to December 1954 in store at Brighton shed but in early 1955 they moved on to other depots. *KRP - 119F.5.*

Before we leave the precincts of Ashford and its engine shed in July 1954, we will have a last look at veteran 0-6-0, No.31064, one of the few remaining Stirling O1 tender engines still working at this time. Admitted, this was another of Wainwright's rebuilds from an older design but he did a good job giving the rebuilds a dome. A total of fifty-eight of the original 115 Class O engines were rebuilt and most of those became BR property. Condemnations had however, by July 1954, eaten steadily into their number and only eight were still active. No.31064 had been on the Ashford strength since July 1951 when it had transferred from Bricklayers Arms. Other members of the class were allocated to either Ashford or Dover sheds, as had been the case since July 1951 when Bricklayers Arms, Faversham, Hither Green and Ramsgate all lost their single examples. In June 1957 No.31064 and 31048 transferred to Stewarts Lane where No.31064 ended its working days in May 1958, if not before unofficially. No.31948 moved on to Nine Elms of all places but returned to the South Eastern section in early 1960 to work its last days from Dover shed. *KRP - 10H.8.1.*

NEW ROMNEY

In September 1960 it was still possible to catch a train at Ashford and travel down to the coast at New Romney. In the summer of 1956 you could get a direct service from Charing Cross (11.30 a.m.) via Ashford and on 28th July 1956 Redhill based BR Standard Cl.4 No.76060 piloted Tonbridge allocated U1 No.31910 from Ashford to Lydd Town from where the Standard then worked a military special. That working was possibly the first time that a Cl.4 Standard 2-6-0 had worked over the line. The journey from Ashford to New Romney was via Ham Street & Orlestone, and Appledore (the one in Kent!) where a change in direction took the train from the Hastings line onto the Dungeness branch. On then through Brookland (opened December 1881, closed March 1967), Lydd Town (also opened December 1881 and closed March 1967), another change of direction, first east, then due north along the coast from Lydd-on-Sea, then Greatstone-on-Sea (both opened July 1937, and closed March 1967), finally reaching the end of the line at New Romney & Littlestone-on-Sea, 13½ miles from Appledore. The terminus here was opened in June 1884 by the South Eastern and was initially called New Romney & Littlestone. Four years later '-on-Sea' was added to the name perhaps to attract passengers from the hinterland wanting a day by the sea. In 1937 the Southern Railway abandoned the original 1881/84 alignment from Lydd Town to New Romney and built a new line through Lydd-on-Sea which took a more southerly curve to reach the coast sooner (Dungeness was finally cut off from the rest of the network in May 1953 when the final mile of remaining track was lifted). Thus was created stations at Lydd-on-Sea and Greatstone-on-Sea. In 1954 both stations were downgraded to Halt status but remained open for business until the line itself was given up on Monday 6th March 1967. Standing at the terminus in September 1960 with its three-coach train for Ashford, was Ashford based H class 0-4-4T No.31307. Not one of the push-pull members of the class, the four-coupled tank had just uncoupled, run round and is now coupling up for the journey back to Ashford. At this time, early September 1960, Ashford had three H class tanks available for use on this working, the other two being motor fitted. Typically the weather was somewhat damp for a day by the sea. *DHB - 4695.*

A view of the train from the opposite side of the terminus. The grass covered platform on the right, seen to better effect in the previous view, was a goods loading bank which had been left to its own devices over the years of disuse. The goods yard proper was beyond the platform fence. The barley twist gas lamp posts had recently acquired new enamel totem nameplates with the station's full title emblazoned. When the H class tanks threw in the towel in 1959, BR Standard Cl.4 tanks began to appear on the branch services but in the haste to rid the Region of steam these too gave way to diesel hauled (Class 24) trains. In the period under review here the 0-4-4 tanks worked nine return trips a day between Appledore and New Romney during the winter service which increased to ten during the summer, with four trains on a Sunday. Diesel-electric multiple units comprised the last motive power used on the branch to its closure. Of course this place was more famous for another railway attraction - the Romney, Hythe & Dymchurch Railway. Opened in 1927, the narrow gauge line is still doing business and attracting the crowds and not just railway enthusiasts either. *DHB - 4694.*

49

APPLEDORE

The junction for the New Romney/Dungeness branch was at Appledore, about seven miles south of Ashford, and here was an extensive goods yard which, in 1960, got a new lease of life with the building of the nuclear power station at Dungeness. Dungeness terminus and the short branch line to that place was abandoned in 1937 when the new alignment to Lydd-on-Sea was brought into use. The wide expanse of open country around this place did not make for happy workers when the weather was inclement but the two gentlemen on the track seemed to be well enough attired for the rain. The crew of the C class 0-6-0 on the other hand are braving the elements as footplatemen had done over the years where inadequate cabs have offered little or no protection to the enginemen. It is a wonder that the railways got away with it for so long and was it any wonder that the BR Standard classes were welcomed with such enthusiasm wherever they ended up. No.31255 is on a trip working from Ashford and sorting out various wagons before the crew can go home. Note the former locomotive tender on the right DS70009 which is now used as a water carried and is labelled *For Drinking Water Only LYDD TOWN*. Although a haven for wildlife, Romney Marsh did not offer much shelter for humans and to this day it remains one of South's less hospitable but nevertheless superb natural wilderness areas. *DHB - 4692.*

Still raining at Appledore as the C class heads towards the goods shed after releasing its train. The place seemed to have all the necessary facilities for a village out in the middle of nowhere (the village had a population of 600 or so, and was situated 1½ miles from the railway station). Besides the goods shed there was a 1½ ton capacity hand crane for those heavy awkward pieces, a landing for horse boxes and of course the livestock pens alongside the shed. Note that the station platforms are staggered. Who is that shadowy figure stood next to the tree in the left background - the Station Master perhaps - watching proceedings. Being the Station Master at Appledore would also put the man in charge of the branch to New Romney, but more importantly the resurrected branch to Dungeness now that construction of the power station was underway, so his importance will have been elevated somewhat with the construction traffic using the branch line and his yard. So, take your mind back fifty years or so to 1960. It was a fairly warm period in the Cold War and the security of Britain's strategic assets was paramount, power stations under construction included, especially the nuclear ones. Now this place had been in the 'front line' just twenty years previously from a different enemy and once again the local officials were asked to do their bit and a little extra too. In certain parts of the country people with cameras were viewed with suspicion (isn't that still in force at railway stations?), so, the SM's vigilance seems appropriate in the circumstances. There again, it might have been somebody waiting for a bus! For the record, the 410 MW Dungeness 'A' power station became fully operation in 1965 but somebody had laid a 200 kV capacity cable from the nuclear facility, then beneath the English Channel to France. So all the vigilance was for nought - they had sneaked into the sea taking the electricity with them! *DHB - 4691.*

51

Looking like an evacuee from a scrapyard, Tonbridge based Q1 class No.33035 heads through Appledore with a mixed freight in September 1960. No matter what emotions their austere appearance might conjure, the Q1 cab was a reasonable place to be on a day such as this. Nearly half of the Q1 class (18) were allocated to Tonbridge at this time; Feltham had twelve whilst Guildford could muster four. Eastleigh and Nine Elms had three each. Their place at Hither Green was now taken by the increasing fleet of diesels. The station platform is a joy to behold, even in the rain, its tended flower beds and overhanging foliage complementing the barley twist (spiral) design of the gas lamps. Note the signals for the main line and branch; the various crossovers effecting movement to both platforms from the branch line. Opened in February 1851, Appledore (Kent) station is still open for business. The route from Ashford is still two-track but westwards to Hastings it is singled. As for the branch to Dungeness nuclear power station - that too is still open for business and probably will be for the next ten thousand years or so, give or take a millennium. *DHB - 4693.*

FOLKESTONE

Dover based Class R 0-4-4T No.31661 was living on borrowed time by July 1954 and here at Folkestone Junction depot on the 26th of that month the veteran is far from busy. Built in 1891, No.31661 became the penultimate member of its class and was one of five which entered BR ownership not to have been fitted with push-pull equipment. It was outlived by No.31666 (featured elsewhere in this album) by just three months, being condemned in September 1955. *KRP - 9H.8.8.*

In 1956, as it had been doing since 1952, the southbound *GOLDEN ARROW* took its Paris-bound passengers to Folkestone harbour but the London-bound passengers arriving in England disembarked at Dover. This meant that the locomotive hauling the Down train would detach at Folkestone Junction and the Pullman cars making up the train were hauled down to the harbour by the resident R1 0-6-0 tank engines. During the period that the passenger stock was being unloaded and its reappearance at the Junction yard, the Pacific was turned, coaled and watered at Folkestone Junction engine shed. Hence the reason for the bulk of 'Merchant Navy' No.35026 LAMPORT & HOLT LINE hogging the shed throat at the small three-road depot in July 1956. Note the fragile looking coal bench with a pile of ghastly looking material, passing itself off as coal, stacked behind. Well that might do the tank engines which ran up and down the incline on the harbour branch umpteen times a day but one of the premier passenger trains on BR would have none of that. So, different arrangements were obviously made for the GA train engine. In this view the Pacific appears to be getting its coal from another, sadly hidden, source although why Stewarts Lane could not put enough decent coal into the tender for a return trip seems illogical in the circumstances. Perhaps 73A did do that and the enginemen were just trimming the coal and bashing some of the bigger pieces. But there are three of them up on the tender? Now, look at the size of that arrow compared with the one gracing the smoke deflector on 'Brit' No.70004 at Victoria. So, once the Pacific has been serviced and the stock brought back to the junction yard, the train engine then couples onto the stock and works tender first to Dover Marine in time to meet the London-bound passengers disembarking from the BR Vessel the Invicta. Running round at Dover put the engine back at the front of the train for the Up journey to Victoria. On arrival in London, at around 6.30 p.m. or thereabouts and with the passengers now going their own way, the stock and train engine were hauled out of Victoria, over the river and into the carriage sidings at Stewarts Lane, the stock going through servicing and then being tucked up for the night whilst the engine went onto 73A for a similar routine. The day after the whole thing started all over again. No wonder the two 'Brits' hung on to the GA job for years before relinquishing to the Bulleid Pacifics in 1958. No matter which way you look at the Stewarts Lane No.4 Duty, it was a cushy one for any locomotive and its crew. DHB - 3487.

Over at the junction in Folkestone on that warm July afternoon in 1956, R1 0-6-0T No.31069 reaches level ground as it hauls the empty Pullman stock of the *GOLDEN ARROW* up the last few yards of the incline from the harbour. Banking assistance was supplied by a sister engine somewhere below wheel level. In 1956 Dover shed, of which Folkestone was a sub-shed, had eight R1 0-6-0 tanks for these short though strenuous feats of haulage. *DHB - 32.*

(*overleaf*) In February 1959 six WR Pannier tanks - Nos.4601, 4610, 4616, 4626, 4630, and 4631 - transferred allegiance to the SR and found themselves at Folkestone Junction shed. They were drawn from sheds in South Wales, namely Abercynon, Barry, and Merthyr. At the same time Nos.4634, 4672, 4681, 4692, and 4698, again drawn from depots in South Wales at Barry, Duffryn Yard, Radyr, made an appearance at Nine Elms - coincidence or a WR covert operation to take over even more SR territory. Only the former engines interest us here - the latter five will be reviewed in a later album in the series - and, in September 1960 No.4610 is seen in the yard at Folkestone Junction awaiting its next job. On their arrival, the WR engines ousted the seven remaining ancient R1 0-6-0 tank engines allocated to the 73H (Dover's new shed code) sub. Co-incidentally the R1s were transferred out of the Eastern Section to Nine Elms shed but their fortunes rapidly diminished and over the next twelve months all of them had been condemned. In April 1960 another Pannier, No.3633, arrived at the Junction shed; this one was also ex Valleys but had come to Kent via Wadebridge and Exmouth Junction. So, the Panniers settled down to their new job but amidst much criticism, not least from the SR Authorities who were peeved at getting, in their believe, mechanically unsound engines. The appearance of No.3633 was probably to placate the irate parties as its timely transfer fitted nicely with the timescales involved. Within no time the Panniers were receiving General overhauls at Eastleigh works. Now at this time other events taking place on the SR were that the Bulleid Pacifics were still being rebuilt, the BR Std. Cl.5s were still receiving Arthurian names whilst 'Schools' were being withdrawn. However, the employment of WR 0-6-0PT on the Folkestone Harbour branch was to be short lived as electrification made them redundant. Their shed closed 12th June 1961 and they moved away to the London area but staying on the Region; much later they dispersed into WR territory - their mission a failure. Note the wall constructed from briquettes - it was about all they were useful for. DHB - 4697.

After exiting Martello tunnel, Bricklayers Arms based 'Schools' No.30931 KING'S-WIMBLEDON approaches Folkestone Junction with an Up boat train in July 1956. This engine was the first of the class to appear in the lined black British Railways livery but it later reverted to green, albeit the lined BR Brunswick style. The spur going off picture to the left led to the engine shed whilst the yard on the right, overlooked by the large Peek Frean advertisement on the somewhat elaborate hoarding, was used to shuffle the boat trains which used the harbour branch. The advertising hoarding did have a twin at the south end of Lewes station but it was pushing Booth's Gin rather than biscuits. *DHB - 104.*

'Schools' No.30935 SEVENOAKS sets back into the junction yard to pick-up vehicles for London in September 1960. Already the yard is quite busy with other coaching stock requiring attention and a single Pannier shuffling about the place. Note the third-rail laid out and boxed for safety. The main line has yet to receive its conductor rails but the station is getting a new Up platform along with a luggage bridge. Just through the arch formed by the new bridge can be seen the south wall of the engine shed. One of the PTs is busy on the right. *DHB - 4704.*

With steam to spare, it seems, Rebuilt 'West Country' No.34021 DARTMOOR runs through Folkestone with a Dover bound train in September 1960. One of the early rebuilds, coming into traffic in December 1957, the Pacific is now part of the Bricklayers Arms allocation and can't you tell. A semblance of calm has now settled over the junction and once the 'WC' has gone through there will be a lull for a couple of hours before it all erupts once again. As for the builders, we can only assume it is another Sunday! *DHB - 4706.*

DOVER

We are at the base of Shakespeare cliff on Monday 16th July 1956 as the six-coach Royal Train approaches with superbly turned-out 'West Country' Pacific No.34092 CITY OF WELLS, of Stewarts Lane, heading towards London (Victoria) with King Feisal of Iraq and the Duke of Gloucester aboard. The Duke had arrived in Dover to escort the King in another special headed by 'Schools' No.30925 CHELTENHAM. How did 73A get those buffer heads so immaculate? Evidence of the continuing battle between the railways and nature are evident in this view which shows the inactive and somewhat neglected construction site. *DHB - 35.*

Beyer, Peacock built L class 4-4-0 No.31761 exits Shakespeare tunnel with a three-coach 'stopper' from Ashford to Dover on 16th July 1956. The massive portals of the tunnel are themselves dwarfed by the towering cliffs at this seemingly precarious location on the very edge of England. Since its opening in 1844, the main line between Dover and Folkestone has, at varying times, been subject to landslip whereby the cliff tries to meet the sea. The problem is most acute at the western end of the stretch at Folkestone Warren and two 'slips' during the 20th century resulted in the main line being closed for considerable periods of time. The first occurred in 1915 and that event closed the line until 1919, causing disruption at a most inconvenient period in British history. The next slippage took place over a slow period during 1936/37 and prompted the Southern to do something other than repair work to the area. In 1938 deep boreholes were driven into the Warren and science was brought into play. It was found that water lying between two solid masses, simply put as one above the other, was causing the upper mass to move under certain conditions. Get rid of the water and you get rid of the problem was the short answer. BR then took on the responsibility and besides drilling boreholes to find further sources of the problem, they began digging drainage tunnels beneath the Warren and, in some places, beneath the high cliffs themselves. To counter the sea trying its best to scour the land beneath the railway line and further de-stabilise the whole lot, massive concrete walls were constructed and to this day the remedial work continues. Mineral wagons, loaded with coal for Dover engine shed, stable on the track adjacent to the sea wall. This line of wagons sometimes stretched all the way back to the shed some quarter mile distant. *DHB - 98.*

It was a long time ago when this E5 was carrying the name HOLLINGTON and working semi-fast main line passenger trains for the London, Brighton & South Coast Railway. It is now 26th July 1954 and the 0-6-2T is relegated to what appears to be the shed steam heating role at Dover motive power depot. The pipe leading off to goodness knows where, is semi-rigid and is obviously of 'local ' design but is neither inconspicuous nor tidy. The coal wagon behind supplied coal for the engine's bunker and whoever looked-after that department had plenty of hefty chucking to perform. How long the E5 stood in this position alongside the main line and performed this particular role is unknown but it was condemned in January 1956, eighteen months hence. Coincidentally the other two members of the class, No.32571 at Norwood Junction and No.32583 at Basingstoke, were condemned at the same time therefore making Class E5 extinct. No.32593 went to Ashford works and was cut up there. Note rather filthy 'BB' No.34072 257 SQUADRON stabled alongside. The Pacific had been working from Dover shed since it was put into traffic at Brighton works in April 1948 and it still had another four years service at 74C before transferring to Exmouth Junction at the end of February 1958. Never rebuilt, No.34072 was withdrawn in October 1964 and is now one of the preserved examples of the class. *KRP - 9H.8.3.*

So, how many Pacifics do you need for these boat trains? Dover shed yard July 1956 with two 'Battle of Britain' on view along with 'Merchant Navy' No.35021 NEW ZEALAND LINE, left, along with lesser mortals (one of Ashford's Fairburn 2-6-4 tank, No.42097 stands alongside the 'MN'). 'BB' No.34078 KENLEY is hogging centre stage with No.34085 501 SQUADRON on the coaling road to its right. It was certainly busy and cramped at Dover during certain periods of the day and this appears to be one of those periods. The depot here was created during 1928 and 1929 on reclaimed land adjacent to the 'high water mark' south of the main line. A tunnel over the main line was removed during the construction. A five road shed, built in concrete (what else) and to the northlight design, was erected. By now the Southern had adopted the London & South Western all concrete shed as employed at Feltham and Exmouth Junction. A turntable, coaling stage and water softener completed the facilities. Note the double-slip, a piece of trackwork rare at any locomotive depot but which was a sure sign of the cramped conditions inherent at this place. The two Light Pacifics were both from Stewarts Lane depot but No.35021 was at this time allocated to Nine Elms shed so it can only be assumed it was on loan to 73A. A note about No.34085; although put into traffic in November 1948, it did not carry any nameplates until after November 1953 and was probably fitted with the plates at its March/April 'General' at Eastleigh in 1954. DHB - 85.

'Schools' No.30919 HARROW catches the last rays of the evening sun at Dover in July 1956. The shed building by this time was looking none too clever but it would only have to last out for another five years before its services were no longer required. closing on 12th June 1961, it outlasted this 4-4-0 by four months. It is often forgotten that two separate companies once ran their own boat trains to this place and in a bid to have their passengers settled on the same Calais bound steamer first, each company - London, Chatham & Dover from Victoria and the South Eastern from Charing Cross - pulled out all the stops with the SER using their route from Ashford through Folkestone and the Chatham lot coming in from the north of the town. The distances involved from London were virtually the same but gradients were not, however, it was usually a very even finish by seconds or minutes. In his History of the Southern Railway Dendy Marshall quotes from an amusing press cutting from circa 1865, which is worth an airing once again because it sums up nicely the rivalries between the railways in the UK: - *'It is generally a moot point whether the express from Charing Cross or Victoria shall be the first alongside the steamer at Dover. The fact has been noted by the idlers on the pier, who have devised a new form of gambling, and bets are freely laid as to which train shall be the first past the post.....the betting is accordingly even. When the signals have fallen on both tracks the excitement becomes intense. The S.E.R. has a clear run in by the shore and when the train shoots out of the tunnel the backers of Charing Cross are jubilant; but, as often as not, Victoria suddenly shoots round the corner and wins...'* Those were the days. DHB - 101.

Wainwright 2F C class 0-6-0 No.31191 shunts a train of Continental wagons at Dover Marine in July 1956. It is often forgotten how much in the way of foreign goods came into the country, during the Fifties, through Dover and the train ferries serving the port. This view gives a reasonable idea of the number of wagons to be seen passing through the port at any one time. Of course these usually went further inland by way of Hither Green yard where they would be sorted by ultimate destination. From there various trip workings would disperse the wagons to the likes of Willesden, Ferme Park and Stratford, where further sorting would put them into northbound workings approximating their eventual destination. Once the wagon had been relieved of its contents it would be either loaded with European bound goods or worked back through the same routes to eventually end up at Dover ready for the short crossing of the Channel. The whole process on the British side might take up to a month and so involved a lot of vehicles. What time it took south of Calais is anyone's guess. It was little wonder then that the Channel Tunnel was required, if only to cut down on the wagon requirement. Nowadays these long forgotten scenes at least remind us of our dependency on overseas produce and goods, even then. *DHB - 99.*

Here is another of those Class P 0-6-0 tank engines which are popular with preservationists, etc. This is the left side of lucky No.31323 at Dover shed in July 1954, included for comparison purposes with the right side of unlucky No.31557 shown earlier. I mention luck because this particular engine was preserved after its July 1960 withdrawal, which incidentally, took place fifty years to the day when these little 0-6-0T was put into traffic from Ashford works. One of three employed at 74C at this time, to work the docks and harbour area, No.31323 had recently returned from a stint with the National Coal Board working at the nearby Snowdown Colliery. At Nationalisation it was possible to find five of the class at Dover, with the other three in the care of Brighton shed. The Class P 0-6-0Ts and the 0-4-0 tanks of Class B4 were apparently the only engines allowed to work the sea-front line during the BR steam era but by June 1957 a Drewry type Robert Stephenson & Hawthorn built 0-6-0 diesel-mechanical shunter, 11220 (later Class 04 D2250) had also taken on work at the docks. In earlier times an A1X had also been employed here, if only briefly. Whenever these engines worked to the Eastern docks, they had to traverse certain of the streets in Dover and in doing so they were preceded by a pilotman with a flag - just like the dawn of the steam railway. *KRP - 9H.8.6.*

BRICKLAYERS ARMS

Returning from whence we started our mini tour of the Southern, we are back in London, but not at one of the stations. Instead we will have a quick look around the grit, grime and delapidation that was Bricklayers Arms engine shed. There is plenty of room on the turntable for 'Schools' No.30917 ARDINGLY as it turns ready for its next working on Saturday 31st December 1955. Still wearing the black lined British Railways livery it will soon revert to a green lined livery befitting its standing in the Southern Region express locomotive fleet. *KRP - 110F.4.* 67

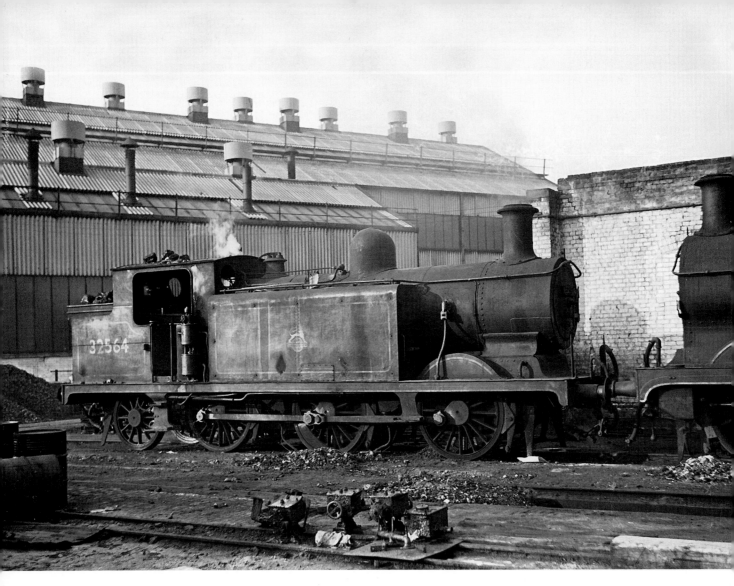

Bricklayers Arms shed was a rambling place consisting running sheds and workshops, the latter capable of handling heavy overhauls. However, in 1955 it was a shadow of its former self and many of the locomotive stabling roads were open to the elements as here where ex LBSCR E4 No.32564 stands on one of the roofless shed roads on Saturday 31st December 1955. The 0-6-2T was standing just to the right of the turntable featured in the previous illustration and in the 'shed' accessed only by the said turntable. That shed was built in 1869 and comprised six covered roads, reduced to four in 1938 but rendered completely roofless by German bombs during WW2. It was known always as the 'New shed' being the last building at the depot built specifically for locomotives purposes. By 1955 it was used mainly for the seasonal storing of out of service locomotives. No.32564 was not in fact stored and was simply using the 'yard' for stabling. The 0-6-2T managed to spend the whole of the fifties working from Bricklayers Arms and only moved to Three Bridges in February 1960 but that transfer was short-lived as the E4 was condemned in September 1961. Typical of the period, ash, clinker and rubbish was strewn everywhere. Even equipment such as the mechanical lubricators in the foreground were left awaiting removal. *KRP - 110F.6.*

D1 No.31739 stables on the threshold of the 1865 extension of the 'Old shed' on New Years Eve 1955. As can be gleaned from this aspect, the original four-road 1847 shed alongside had a new roof which had been erected in 1937 by the Southern Railway in a northlight style, using corrugated materials for cladding. The original brick walls were obviously deemed 'solid' enough to stay. The 1865 shed, also of four roads, was also re-roofed but in a different style and at a different period, by British Railways in 1952. The SR re-roofing design, using, in the main, old rails for the framework, was also used at St Leonards and Tunbridge Wells West along with a few other engine sheds in Kent and Sussex, although this shed did not have the benefit of a brick gable. Note the use of chimneys on the pre-war rebuild whilst the post-war job has done away with them, and the internal smoke troughs. Besides these other two engine sheds, there was another shed at the west end of the depot known as 'St Patricks shed' and also consisting four roads. That particular shed started life as a carriage shed but was converted for locomotives purposes in 1902. It too was re-roofed in 1937 with a northlight structure. The whole depot at Bricklayers Arms was closed in June 1962 and subsequently demolished. *KRP - 110F.2.*

69

Earlier during the morning of 31st December 1955, another 'Schools' No.30907 DULWICH was being got ready for a working from Charing Cross down to Dover. Note that even those locomotives employed on the Regions premier passenger turns were not immune from the dreaded briquettes. Bricklayers Arms motive power depot was sited at the end of a spur, some distance from the main line. Alongside was a large goods depot which in many respects hindered any outward growth on the north side of the site. 'The Brick' as the shed was known locally, was a busy place servicing both passenger and goods engines and any long-term modernisation would have been a nightmare to accomplish even before the Grouping so the patching up and make do and mend of the available facilities was always going to be the order of the day at this place. KRP - 110F.7.

NORWOOD JUNCTION

Being shunted about the place by one of the depot's 350 h.p. diesel-electric shunters, Q class No.30538 is joined by E6 0-6-2T No.32416 at Norwood Junction shed on the last day of 1955. Both engines have had a coat of paint around the boiler areas although it could just as easily have been a good rub-down with a paraffin soaked cloth or two. Norwood Junction engine shed the first on the Southern Region to get a permanent allocation of diesel shunters with seven of the Ashford built (later Class 12) 0-6-0 type arriving there during April, May and June 1949. The diesel allocation grew gradually over the next couple of years so that by December 1951 nineteen various diesels were resident, including the Bulleid one-off diesel-mechanical No.11001 which joined the complement in May 1950. The diesel allocation fluctuated enormously over the next decade with twenty being 'on-the-books' in June 1952 yet only four some three months later. This Q class 0-6-0 had been a resident here for years, along with others - Nos.30533, 30534, 30537, 30539 and 30547 - and the situation remained that way until they were withdrawn. From October 1961 No.30538 was fitted with a BR Standard chimney in place of this straight sided affair. The depot at 75C also housed about five of the E6 class throughout the fifties, with No.32416 arriving from Eastleigh shed in September 1953. That particular 0-6-2T turned out to be the last of the class working from Norwood Junction and transferred to Bricklayers Arms in July 1959. *KRP - 111F.5.*

The C2X 0-6-0 was another pre-Grouping class familiar with Norwood Junction shed and on 31st December 1955 No.32547 was caught reversing from the coaling stage at the side of the shed after refuelling. Note the vast number of briquettes stacked on the tender - it was a bad time to get decent coal anywhere in the country. Not having to bother with the coaling stage but nevertheless having to use the coaling road, one of the depot's 350 h.p. 0-6-0 diesel shunters is also being refuelled (by gravity) from one of the tank wagons on the elevated stage road. For the diesels, this method of taking on fuel had gone on for some years but now dedicated fuel tanks were being supplied to the depot, and evidence of their foundation is seen in front of the C2X with shuttering in situ for the concrete foundation of a brick-built bund wall. The continuing drought of coal from the National Coal Board during the early fifties was one of the factors which hastened the implementation of the BR Modernisation Plan in 1955 so that resources destined for other equally deserving projects, such as station, signal and track modernisation, were diverted to getting equipment installed for the diesel fleet. *KRP - 111F.2.*